American Art Association

Modern paintings comprising the two private collections

formed by Elmer H. Capen

American Art Association

Modern paintings comprising the two private collections formed by Elmer H. Capen

ISBN/EAN: 9783744646611

Printed in Europe, USA, Canada, Australia, Japan

Cover: Foto ©Thomas Meinert / pixelio.de

More available books at **www.hansebooks.com**

No. 157 Maude   A   mother.

ILLUSTRATED CATALOGUE

OF

MODERN PAINTINGS

COMPRISING THE

TWO PRIVATE COLLECTIONS

FORMED BY

ELMER H. CAPEN, OF BOSTON

AND THE LATE

WILMOT L. WARREN, OF SPRINGFIELD, MASS

THE TWO COLLECTIONS TO BE SOLD

BY AUCTION, WITHOUT RESERVE

AT CHICKERING HALL

FIFTH AVENUE AND EIGHTEENTH STREET

THURSDAY AND FRIDAY EVENINGS, MARCH 7TH AND 8TH

BEGINNING PROMPTLY AT 8 O'CLOCK EACH EVENING

THE PAINTINGS WILL BE ON PUBLIC EXHIBITION
DAY AND EVENING

AT THE AMERICAN ART GALLERIES

6 AND 8 EAST TWENTY-THIRD STREET, MADISON SQUARE

FROM FRIDAY, FEBRUARY 22D, UNTIL DAY OF SALE INCLUSIVE
(SUNDAYS EXCEPTED)

AMERICAN ART ASSOCIATION, MANAGERS

THOMAS E. KIRBY, AUCTIONEER

NEW YORK, 1889

1. The highest Bidder to be the Buyer, and if any dispute arise between two or more Bidders, the Lot so in dispute shall be immediately put up again and re-sold.

2. The Purchasers to give their names and addresses, and to pay down a cash deposit, or the whole of the Purchase-money *if required*, in default of which the Lot or Lots so purchased to be immediately put up again and re-sold.

3. The Lots to be taken away at the Buyer's Expense and Risk *upon the conclusion of the Sale*, and the remainder of the Purchase-money to be absolutely paid, or otherwise settled for to the satisfaction of the Auctioneer, on or before delivery ; in default of which the undersigned will not hold themselves responsible if the Lots be lost, stolen, damaged, or destroyed, but they will be left at the sole risk of the Purchaser.

4. *The sale of any article is not to be set aside on account of any error in the description, or imperfection. All articles are exposed for Public Exhibition one or more days, and are sold just as they are without recourse.*

5. To prevent inaccuracy in delivery and inconvenience in the settlement of the purchases, no Lot can, on any account, be removed during the sale.

6. Upon failure to comply with the above conditions, the money deposited in part payment shall be forfeited ; all Lots uncleared within three days from conclusion of sale shall be re-sold by public or private Sale, without further notice, and the deficiency (if any) attending such re-sale shall be made good by the defaulter at this Sale, together with all charges attending the same. This Condition is without prejudice to the right of the Auctioneer to enforce the contract made at this Sale, without such re-sale, if he thinks fit.

THOS. E. KIRBY,

AUCTIONEER.

INDEX TO ARTISTS REPRESENTED.

BONHEUR (JULIETTE) (MME. PEYROL).......... Paris

Born in Paris, 1830. Daughter and pupil of Raymond Bonheur, and assistant of her sister Rosa in the Free School of Design for Young Girls, founded by them in Paris. Medal, 1855.

No. 91—Pastoral Scene .... Page 44
No. 115—Noontide Rest .... " 48

BONHEUR (F. AUGUSTE)................... Deceased

Born in Bordeaux, November 4, 1824. Son and pupil of Raymond Bonheur, who died 1853. Medals, Paris, 1852, 1857, 1859, 1861, and 1863. Chevalier of the Legion of Honor, 1867. Died, February, 1884.

No. 31—Leader of the Flock .... Page 31

BONNINGTON (RICHARD PARKES).......... Deceased

Born in Arnold, near Nottingham, England, 1801. Pupil of Gros. Gold Medal, 1824. His painting, " François Ier et la Duchess d'Étampes," is in the Louvre, Paris. Died, 1828.

No. 99—French Port .... Page 45

BOUDIN (EUGÈNE LOUIS)..................... Paris

Born at Honfleur. Medals, 1881, 1883.

No. 6—Landscape .... Page 26
No. 90—Shipping at Havre .... " 43

BRADFORD (WILLIAM)................. ...New York

Born in New Bedford, Mass , 1830. Self-taught, but influenced by Van Beest, whose studio he shared for two years. Accompanied several Arctic expeditions to study icebergs. Elected A.N.A., 1874.

No. 9—Sunset on the Coast of Labrador............. Page 27
No. 100—Fishing Vessels Among the Icebergs .... " 45

BROWN (George Loring) .... Boston

Born in Boston, 1814. Pupil of Washington Allston, and in Paris of Eugene Isabey. Visited Europe in 1840, and painted in London, Paris, Antwerp, Florence, and Rome. Returned in 1860.

No. 79—Old Fisherman's Home, Amalfi .... Page 41

ABAT (Louis) .... Paris

Born in Paris, 1812. Landscape painter. Pupil of Camille Flers. Medals, 1834, 1867. Chevalier of the Legion of Honor, 1843. Officer of the same, 1855. Member of the Institute, 1867. Director of the French Academy at Rome, 1879.

No. 87—Atalanta .... Page 43

CHASE (William Merritt) .... New York

Born in Franklin, Indiana, 1849. Pupil of B. F. Hayes in Indianapolis, of the National Academy, and of J. O. Eaton, New York. Studied for six years at Munich Academy under Wagner and Piloty. Won Honorable Mention at Salon, Paris, 1882. and Medal at Munich Exposition, 1883. Elected A.N.A., New York, 1883.

No. 85—Brooklyn Heights .... Page 42

LAYS (Paul Jean) .... Brussels

Born, 1819 Pupil in Paris, of Gudin. Medals, Brussels, 1851. Paris, 1867 and 1878. Chevalier of the Legion of Honor, 1875. Officer of the same, 1881. Member of the Order of Leopold.

No. 63—On the Scheldt .... Page 38

COLE (J. Foxcroft) .... Boston

Born in Jay, Maine, 1837. Pupil of Lambinet and of Jacque.

No. 8—Landscape and Sheep .... Page 27
No. 13—Head from Life .... " 28

CONSTABLE (John).....................Deceased

Born in Suffolk, 1776. Died in London, 1837. Landscape painter. Studied at Royal Academy and later with Joseph Farrington and R. R. Reinagle. First exhibited in 1802. Elected A. R. A., 1819, and R. A., 1829. In France he found his first recognition, and is the most highly esteemed of all British painters. He is represented in the Louvre by two fine examples of his work. He exerted great influence upon the modern school of French landscape painting.

COROT (Jean Baptiste Camille).............Deceased

Born in Paris. 1796. Was first instructed by Michallon, after ward by Victor Bertin, then spent several years in Italy. Medals, Paris, 1836, 1848, 1855, 1867 (*Exposition Universelle*). Chevalier of the Legion of Honor, 1846. Officer of the same, 1867. Died, 1875. Diploma to the Memory of Deceased Artists (*Exposition Universelle*), 1878.

COURBET (Gustave)............. ....Deceased

Born in Ornans. 1819. Died, January 1, 1878. He began to study law, but devoted his time to the studios, studying mainly with David d'Angers. He first attracted attention in 1849, when his *Funeral at Ornans*, now in the Louvre, was exhibited. Medals, 1849, 1857, 1861. Was offered the Cross of the Legion of Honor, but refused it. Decorated with the order of St. Michael. As chief instigator of the overthrow of the Column Vendome in Paris during the Commune of 1871, he was sentenced to six months' imprisonment, and to bear the cost of its restoration.

DAUBIGNY (CHARLES FRANÇOIS)............Deceased

Born in Paris, 1817. Pupil of his father and Paul Delaroche, and for three years studied in Italy. Medals, 1848, 1853, 1855, 1857, 1859, 1867. Chevalier of the Legion of Honor, 1859. Officer of the same, 1874 Died, 1878. Diploma to the Memory of Deceased Artists (*Exposition Universelle*), 1878.

DAUBIGNY (KARL-PIERRE)................Deceased

Born, 1846. Son and pupil of C. F. Daubigny. Medals, Salon, 1868, 1874. *Hors Concours.* Died. 1886.

DECAMPS (ALEXANDER GABRIEL ....Deceased

Born in Paris, 1803 Died, 1860. Pupil of Abel de Pujol, David and Ingres. Traveled in the East in 1827, after which he devoted himself to painting Oriental subjects. Medals, 1831, 1834. Chevalier of the Legion of Honor, 1839. Officer of the same, 1851.

Born in Bordeaux, 1809, of parents who had been banished from
Spain on account of political troubles.   At ten years of age Diaz
was left an orphan, and at fifteen he was apprenticed to a maker of
porcelain, where his talent first displayed itself.   He quarreled
with and left his master, and subsequently spent several years in
most bitter poverty.   After his ability as a most wonderful colorist

had been recognized, Diaz painted and sold many pictures, endeavoring, by the accumulation of a fortune, to avenge the poverty of his youth. He died in Paris from the sting of a viper in 1876. Medals in 1844, 1846, 1848. Chevalier of the Legion of Honor, 1851. Diploma to the Memory of Deceased Artists (*Exposition Universelle*), 1878.

DORÉ (GUSTAVE PAUL)............... ......Deceased

Born in Strasburg, 1833. Died in Paris, 1883. Went to Paris when fifteen years of age and began contributing sketches to illustrated periodicals. First exhibited at Salon in 1848. Chevalier of the Legion of Honor, 1861. Officer of the same, 1879. Also showed great ability as a sculptor.

DUPRÉ (LÉON VICTOR .... Deceased

Born in Limoges, 1816. Brother and pupil of Jules Dupré. Medals at Paris, 1849, and Philadelphia, 1876.

DUPRÉ (JULES).............................. ....Paris

Born at Nantes, 1812. When a boy he studied design in the porcelain manufactory of his father, but soon turned his attention to landscape painting, and made his *début* at the Salon, 1831. Medal, 1833. Chevalier of the Legion of Honor, 1849. Medal (*Exposition Universelle*), 1867. Officer of the Legion of Honor, 1870.

FROMENTIN Eugène...................Deceased

Born in La Rochelle in 1820. Died, 1876. Pupil of Rémond
and Cabat. He was the author of a successful romance, also of
several works of art and travel. Medals, 1849. 1857, 1859.
Chevalier of the Legion of Honor, 1859. Officer of the same, 1869.

FULLER (George.......................Deceased

Born at Deerfield, Mass., 1822. Died in Boston, 1884. Studied
in Boston, New York. and London. Traveled on the Continent.
Elected A. N. A., 1853. Memorial Exhibition of his works was
held at Museum of Fine Arts, Boston, 1884.

GABRIEL (Paul Joseph Constantine).

GÉRICAULT (Jean Louis André Théodore). Deceased

Born in Rouen, 1791. Died at Paris, 1824. Pupil of Carle
Vernet and of Guérin. In 1817, after serving in the army for
three years, he went to Italy and studied in Rome and Florence.
His *Raft of the Medusa*, now in the Louvre, was loudly denounced
by the critics. but its exhibition in London brought the artist a
small fortune, and, on his return to Paris, a Gold Medal.

GÉRÔME (Jean Léon).......................Paris

Born at Vesoul, France, 1824. Went to Paris in 1841, and
entered the studio of Paul Delaroche, at the same time following
the course of *l'École des Beaux Arts*. In 1844 he accompanied
Delaroche to Italy. He made his *début* at the Salon of 1847. In

1853 and 1856 he traveled in Egypt and Turkey, studying closely the history and customs of those countries. Medals, Paris, 1847. 1848, 1855 (*Exposition Universelle*). Medal of the Institute, 1865. Medal of Honor (*Exposition Universelle*), 1867. Medals of Honor, 1874. Medal for Sculpture and one of the eight Grand Medals of Honor (*Exposition Universelle*), 1878. Chevalier of the Legion of Honor, 1855. Officer of the same, 1867. Commander, 1878. Chevalier of the *Order de l'Aigle Rouge*, and member of the Institute of France, 1878. Professor in *l'École des Beaux Arts*.

No. 104—Quintus Curtius .... Page 46

GUDIN (Jean Antoine Théodore) ....Paris

Born in Paris, 1802. Pupil of Girodet-Trioson. Medal, 1824. Chevalier of the Legion of Honor, 1828. Officer of the same, 1841. Commander of the same, 1855. Medals, 1848, 1855 (*Exposition Universelle*).

No. 25—Marine .... Page 30

GUILLAUMET (Gustave) ....Paris

Born in Paris, 1840. Pupil of Picot, Barrias, and *l'École des Beaux Arts*. *Prix de Rome*, 1863. Medals, 1865, 1867, 1872, 1878. Chevalier of the Legion of Honor, 1878.

No. 123—In the Vosges .... Page 50

HEADE (Martin J.) .... New York

Born in Pennsylvania. Studied two years in Italy, and sketched in South America. While in Brazil he was decorated as Chevalier of the Order of the Rose by the Emperor.

No. 78—Lake George .... Page 41

HEREAU (Jules) ....Deceased

Born in Paris, 1830. Died, 1879. Landscape painter of great merit. Medals, 1865-1868.

No. 29—Landscape .... Page 31

HUNT (WILLIAM MORRIS) ....Deceased

Born in Brattleborough, Vt., 1824. Died at the Isles of Shoals, 1879. Studied at Düsseldorf Academy in 1846 with a view to becoming a sculptor. Later he studied in Paris under Couture, and then went to Barbizon to study with Millet, who influenced his work through life. Returned to America in 1855, and opened a studio in Newport, and a little later settled permanently in Boston. Visited Paris again in 1867.

INNESS (GEORGE), N. A...................New York

Born at Newburg, N. Y., 1825. Studied art in Newark, N. J., and engraving in New York. In 1846 began landscape painting as a profession, spending a month meanwhile in the studio of Regis Gignoux. Visited Europe several times for purposes of observation and study, and lived in Italy from 1871 to 1875. Elected National Academician, 1868. Member of the Society of American Artists.

ISABEY (LOUIS EUGÈNE)...................Deceased

Born in Paris, 1804. Died, 1886. Pupil of his father. Medals, 1824, 1827, 1855. Chevalier of the Legion of Honor, 1832. Officer of the same, 1852.

JACQUE (CHARLES ÉMILE)............... ...Paris

Born at Paris, 1813. Early in life studied with a geographical engraver. Later, spent seven years in the army, and worked two years in England as an engraver on wood. Is famous for his etchings as well as his paintings. Medals, Paris. 1861, 1863, 1864, 1867. Chevalier of the Legion of Honor, 1867.

KAULBACH FRIEDRICH AUGUST............Munich

Born in Hanover, 1850. Son and pupil of Friedrich Kaulbach, afterward of Kreling at Nuremberg. Gold Medal at Berlin, 1884. Member of Berlin Academy. Chevalier of the Order of the Crown of Bavaria, 1885. Gold Medals at Munich and Vienna.

KLUMSCH (PROF. EUGÈNE)...... ....Munich

AMBINET (ÉMILE) ....:.Deceased

Born at Versailles, 1810. Pupil of Drölling. Medals, Paris, 1843, 1853, 1857. Chevalier of the Legion of Honor, 1867. Died, 1878.

LATOUCHE (LOUIS) ....Deceased

Born in Fort-sous-Jovarre. Studied in Paris. Died, 18—.

LAWRENCE (SIR THOMAS) .... Deceased

Born in Bristol, 1769. Died in London, 1830. Studied at the Royal Academy and became painter in ordinary to George III. Elected R. A. in 1794. Knighted by the King in 1815, and five years later was elected President of the Royal Academy. Chevalier of the Legion of Honor, 1825. Member of the Academy of St. Luke, Rome, and other foreign academies.

LE ROUX (HECTOR) .... Paris

Born in Verdun, December 29, 1829. Pupil of Picot Medals, Paris, 1863, 1864, 1874. Chevalier of the Legion of Honor, 1877. Medal (*Exposition Universelle*), 1878. His best-known picture, "The Vestal Tuccia." is in the Corcoran Gallery in Washington.

LINDENSCHMITT (PROF. WILHELM) .... Munich

Born in Munich, 1829. Pupil of his father and of the Munich Academy. Also studied in Frankfort, Antwerp, and Paris. Settled in Munich in 1863, when he became Professor in the Academy. Member Berlin Academy. Gold Medal. Berlin, 1870.

MAGNUS (CAMILLE) .... Paris

Pupil of Diaz.

MARILHAT (Prosper) ....Deceased

Born at Vertaizon, 1811. Died there, 1847. Landscape painter, pupil of Roqueplan Visited the East in 1831, and remained in Cairo a number of years, where the climate so ruined his health that he did not long enjoy the fame which awaited him on his return to Paris.

MEISSONIER (Jean Louis Ernest ....Paris

Born at Lyons. 1815. Pupil of Léon Cogniet. First became known as an illustrator of books. Medals, 1840, 1841, 1843, 1848, 1855, 1867, 1878. Chevalier of the Legion of Honor, 1846. Officer of the same, 1856. Commander, 1867. Grand Officer, 1878. Member of the Institute, 1861. Member Munich Academy, 1867. Royal Academy, London.

MÉLIN (Joseph)...............................Deceased

Born at Paris, Feb. 14, 1814. Died, 1887. Pupil of Paul Delaroche and David d'Angers. Medals. 1843, 1855, and 1858.

MEYER (Johann Georg).... ... .Deceased

Called, from his birthplace, Meyer Von Bremen. Born October 28, 1813. Pupil of Sohn. Member of the Amsterdam Academy. Gold Medal of Prussia, 1850. Medals at Berlin and Philadelphia.

2

MICHALLON (Achille Etna)..............Deceased

> Born in Paris, 1796. Died 1822. Son of the sculptor Claude Michallon, and pupil of David, Bertin, and Danouy. Won Medal, 1812, when only sixteen Studied four years in Rome. Won the *Grand Prix* in 1817. Died when only 26 years of age.

MICHEL (Georges) ....Deceased

> Born 1763. Died 1843.

MILLET (Jean François)...................Deceased

> Born at Greville, France, 1814. Pupil of Langlois at Cherbourg. The Municipality of Cherbourg gave him a small pension that he might go to study in Paris. Became pupil of Paul Delaroche in 1837, and the friend of Corot, Rousseau, Dupré, and Diaz. Medals, Paris, 1853, 1864, 1867 (*Exposition Universelle*). Chevalier of the Legion of Honor, 1868. Died, 1875. Diploma to the Memory of Deceased Artists, 1878.

MOLITOR (P.)...........................Rome

MONTICELLI (Adolphe)..................Deceased

> Born in Marseilles, 1824. Pupil of Ramond Aubert and of Diaz. Died at Paris, 1886.

MORVILLIER

No. 77—Landscape .... Page 40

PASINI (ALBERTO) ....Paris

Born at Busseto, Italy. Pupil of Ciceri. Medals, Paris, 1859, 1863, 1864. Grand Medal of Honor (*Exposition Universelle*), 1878. Chevalier of the Legion of Honor, 1868. Officer of the same, 1878. Medal at Vienna Exposition, 1873. Knight of the Order of Saints Maurice and Lazarus, and Officer of the Orders of Turkey and Persia. Honorary Professor of the Academies of Parma and Turin.

No. 4—Coast of Algiers............ .... Page 26
No. 40—On the Coast............................... " 33

PERRAULT (LÉON) ....Paris

Pupil of Picot and Bouguereau. Medals, Salon, 1864, 1876. Chevalier of the Legion of Honor, 1887.

No. 156—The Mendicants.... .... Page 57

PLASSAN (ANTOINE ÉMILE) ....Paris

Born in Bordeaux. Medals, 1852, 1857, 1859. Chevalier of the Legion of Honor, 1859.

No. 3—Landscape .... Page 26
No. 117—Mother and Child........................ " 49

RICO (MARTIN) ....Paris

Born in Madrid. Pupil of Madrazo. Medal at *Exposition Universelle*, 1878. Chevalier of the Legion of Honor, 1878.

No. 45—Landscape .... Page 34

ROBINSON (Thomas) .... Deceased

Born in Nova Scotia, 1835. Pupil of Courbet, and received some instruction from August Bonheur.

ROTHERMEL (Peter F.) .... Philadelphia

Born in Pennsylvania, 1817. History painter. Began painting portraits without tuition in 1840. In 1856 visited Europe for purposes of study and observation. Has since lived in Philadelphia. Is an associate of Pennsylvania Academy.

ROUSSEAU (P. E. Théodore) .... Deceased

Born at Paris. 1812. Pupil of Lethiere. Showed himself a naturalist from the first, and for thirteen years was excluded from the Salon by an Academic jury. First exhibited in 1834. Medals 1834, 1849, 1855. Chevalier of the Legion of Honor, 1852. One of the Eight Grand Medals of Honor (Exposition Universelle), Paris, 1867. Died, 1867. Diploma to the Memory of Deceased Artists, 1878.

SCHENCK (August Frederic Albrecht) .... Paris

Born at Glückstadt, Holstein, 1828. Studied in Paris under Leon Cogniet. Medals, Paris, 1865; Philadelphia, 1876. Chevalier of the Orders of Christ of Portugal, and of Isabella the Catholic.

SCHEFFER (Ary)........................Deceased

Born in Dordrecht, 1795. Pupil of Guérin. Grand Prize for painting at Antwerp, 1816. Medals, Paris, 1824, 1832. Chevalier of the Legion of Honor, 1837. Died, 1858.

STADEMANN (Adolf)....................Munich

Born at Munich, 1824. Pupil of Munich Academy.

TERRY ——)

TOURNEMINE (Charles Émile Vacher de). Deceased

Born in Toulon, 1813. Pupil of Eugène Isabey. Chevalier of the Legion of Honor, 1853. Died, 1872.

TROYON (Constantine).... ....Deceased

Born at Sevres, 1810. Died, 1865. Pupil of Rivereux. Medals, 1838, 1840, 1848, 1855. Chevalier of the Legion of Honor, 1849. Member of the Academy of Amsterdam. Diploma to the Memory of Deceased Artists, 1878.

VAN MARCKE (Émile) ....Paris

Born at Sevres, 1827. Pupil of Troyon. Medals, 1867, 1869, 1870, 1878. Chevalier of the Legion of Honor, 1872.

No. 143—Study of a Cow .... Page 54

VERNET (Émile Jean Horace)............Deceased

Born in Paris, 1789. Died there, 1863 Son and pupil of Carle Vernet. When fifteen years old he supported himself by his drawings. Medal, 1812. Chevalier of the Legion of Honor, 1814. Member of the Institute, 1826. From 1828 to 1839, Director of the French Academy at Rome. Officer of the Legion of Honor, 1825. Commander of the same, 1842. Grand Officer, 1862. Medal of Honor (*Exposition Universelle*), 1855.

No. 66—Study of a Horse .... Page 38
No. 145—Head.... ....   "   54

VOLLON (Antoine)...........................Paris

Born at Lyons. Pupil of Ribot. Medals, 1865, 1868, 1869, 1878. Chevalier of the Legion of Honor, 1870. Officer of the same, 1878.

No. 39—Old Mill .... Page 33
No. 144—Studio Interior.............................   "   54

WATELIN (Louis Victor)....................Paris

Born in Paris. Pupil of Diaz. Medal, 1876.

No. 22—Landscape.................................. Page 29

WEEKS (Edwin Lord)................ ... .Paris

Born in Boston. Pupil of Bonnat. Honorable Mention, Paris, Salon, 1885.

No. 16—Mosque of Kaid Bey—Tombs of the Mamelukes. Page 28

WILKIE (Sir David)..................... Deceased

> Born in Scotland, 1785. Died at Gibraltar, 1841. Studied at
> Academy, Edinburgh, and at Royal Academy, London. Elected
> A.R.A., 1809, and R.A., 1811.

ZEIM (F. F. G. P.) .... Paris

> Born at Beauns (Côte d'Or), February 25, 1821. Medals at Paris,
> 1851, 1852, 1855. Cross of the Legion of Honor, 1857.

CATALOGUE.

NOTE.—The paintings marked with an asterisk belong to the estate of the late Wilmot L. Warren, of Springfield, Mass.; those not so marked are the exclusive property of Elmer H. Capen, of Boston.

No. 1

ROTHERMEL (PETER F.) . . . . Philadelphia

Isabel and Claudio

11¼ x 9¼

No. 2

DUPRÉ (VICTOR) . . . . Paris

Landscape

5¾ x 11

No. 3

PLASSAN (ANTOINE ÉMILE) .... Paris

* Landscape

8½ x 6¼

No. 4

PASINI (ALBERTO) .... Paris

* Coast of Algiers

8¼ x 14½

No. 5

BOGGS (F. M.) .... Paris

Isigny, Normandy

15 x 22

No. 6

BOUDIN (EUGÈNE LOUIS) .... Paris

Landscape

12 x 15¾

No. 7

KAULBACH (FRIEDRICH AUGUST .... Munich

* The Little Mother

8 x 5¼

No. 8

COLE (J. FOXCROFT)....................Boston

Landscape and Sheep

12 x 18

No. 9

BRADFORD (WM.) ....New York

Sunset on the Coast of Labrador

18 x 30

No. 10

KLUMSCH (PROF. EUGENE).. ....

* Children at Play

19½ x 14½

No. 11

GABRIEL (P. J. C.) .... Paris

Landscape

12 x 19

No. 12

HUNT (W. M.)..........................Deceased

Landscape, November Afternoon

12 x 18

No. 13

COLE (J. FOXCROFT) ....Boston

* Head from Life

14 x 11

No. 14

BEYSCHLAG (JULIUS ROBERT)..........Munich

* Mother and Child

12 x 17

No. 15

MAGNUS (CAMILLE) ....Paris

Flowers

14¾ x 21½

No. 16

WEEKS (EDWIN LORD) ....Paris

Mosque of Kaid Bey—
Tombs of the Mamelukes.

21 x 16

No. 17

SCHENCK (AUGUST FREDERICH)..........Paris

Shepherdess and Flock

16 x 24

No. 19. Faust and Marguerite. N. V. Č. az.

No. 18

MEISSONIER (JEAN LOUIS ERNEST).......Paris

Drawing

No. 19

DIAZ (N. V.)...............................Deceased

Faust and Marguerite

14½ x 10½

(Portrait of the Artist.)

No. 20

DAUBIGNY (KARL PIERRE...........Deceased

Sunset

15¾ x 23

No. 21

GÉRICAULT (J. L. A. T.).... ....Deceased

*White Horse

13 x 16¼

No. 22

WATELIN (LOUIS VICTOR)..................Paris

Landscape

16¾ x 23½

No. 23

MONTICELLI (ADOLPHE) . . . . Deceased

Young Girl

20½ x 16

No. 24

DECAMPS (A. G.) . . . . Deceased

Bay in Algiers

19½ x 13¼

No. 25

GUDIN (JEAN ANTOINE THÉODORE . . . . . . Paris

Marine

11¼ x 15¼

No. 26

HUNT (W. M.) . . . . Deceased

Head

14½ x 12¼

No. 27

GÉRICAULT (J. L. A. T.) . . . . Deceased

Stable Interior

14 x 10¾

No. 28

DIAZ (N. V. . . . . Deceased

* Flowers

16 x 13

No. 29

HEREAU (JULES) . . . . Deceased

Landscape

15½ x 23½

No. 30

JACQUE (CHARLES ÉMILE). . . . . Paris

Sheep in the Fold

7⅓ x 10⅓

No. 31

BONHEUR (F. AUGUSTE). . . . . Deceased

Leader of the Flock

8½ x 11⅓

No. 32

DELACROIX (EUGÈNE) . . . . Deceased

The Bath

8⅓ x 6½

No. 33

DE DREUX (ALFRED).....................Deceased

Running Free

6½ x 8½

No. 34

COURBET (GUSTAVE).... ....Deceased

*Wayside Rest

8 x 6½

No. 35

DE METZ (L'ENFANT)...................... Paris

Children's Concert

8½ x 6

No. 36

DAUBIGNY (C. F.) .... Deceased

*Summer's Day

8¾ x 14

No. 37

HUNT (W. M.).. ....Deceased

Early Twilight

8 x 10¾

No. 38

TROYON (CONSTANTINE)........ ....Deceased

Landscape and Sheep

13 x 10

No. 39

VOLLON (ANTOINE). ....Paris

Old Mill

9 x 15

No. 40

PASINI (ALBERTO)...........................Paris

On the Coast

9½ x 14

No. 41

LATOUCHE (LOUIS).....................Deceased

Peasant's Cottage

5½ x 10½

No. 42

MEYER VON BREMEN....................Deceased

Head

5½ x 4½

3

No. 43

LAWRENCE SIR THOMAS`............Deceased

Portrait, Lady with a Guitar

10¼ x 8

No. 44

ROUSSEAU (THÉODORE).... ....Deceased

Alpine Study

6 x 13¾

No. 45

RICO (MARTIN DIEGO ....Paris

* Landscape

9½ x 9½

(From Vibert sale.)

No. 46

MILLET (J. F.......... ....Deceased

Gleaner

10¾ x 8½

No. 47

TROYON (CONSTANTINE)...............Deceased

* Cow Feeding

(Water-Color.)

No. 48

MILLET (J. F.)...................... ..Deceased

* Peasant Gathering Wood

(Pastel.)

No. 49

ROUSSEAU (THÉODORE...... ....Deceased

View at Macon

10¼ x 17¾

No. 50

COROT J. B. C. ....Deceased

* Rocks at Fontainebleau

14 x 20

No. 51

DAUBIGNY (C. F.)......................Deceased

Landscape, Sunset

15 x 26¼

No. 52

COURBET (GUSTAVE...................Deceased

On the Stream

16¾ x 24

No. 53

DECAMPS (A. G.)....... ....Deceased

Dogs

(Bought at the Sale of Lambinet's effects, who had acquired it at
the Decamps Sale.)

13½ x 13½

No. 54

ROBINSON (THOMAS)....................Deceased

Cow

10 x 13½

No. 55

MICHALLON (ACHILLE ETNA)..........Deceased

Landscape

14½ x 18½

No. 56

DIAZ (N. V.).............................Deceased

Behind the Scenes

14 x 10½

No. 57

TOURNEMINE (C. ÉMILE VACHER de).......Paris

The

12½ x 21

No. 58

JACQUE (CHARLES ÉMILE)..................Paris

* Farm-Yard

18 x 15

No. 59

DUPRÉ (JULES)...........................Paris

Autumn Landscape

20 x 29½

No. 60

INNESS (GEORGE)................. ....New York

* Roman Landscape

18 x 26 (dated Rome, 1873)

No. 61

ROBINSON (THOMAS)...................Deceased

Landscape and Cattle

18 x 24

No. 62

MICHEL (GEORGES)......... ....Deceased

Autumn Landscape

20½ x 23¾

No. 63

CLAYS (P. J.)..............................Brussels

*On the Scheldt

16¼ x 24

No. 64

HUNT (W. M.)........................Deceased

The Amazon

24 x 14

No. 65

MARILHAT (PROSPER)..................Deceased

Camel

21½ x 25¾

No. 66

VERNET (HORACE)................ ....Deceased

*Study of a Horse

25¾ x 32

No. 67

ZIEM (FELIX)........ ....Paris

*Venice

16¼ x 28¼

No. 68

COROT (J. B. C.) .... Deceased

Wood Interior

26 x 17

No. 69

DAUBIGNY (C. F.)................... . Deceased

Landscape

8¼ x 14¼

(From the collection of Lavoronat, engraver of Daubigny's principal works.)

No. 70

ROUSSEAU (THÉODORE .... Deceased

Rocks at Fontainebleau

10¼ x 14

No. 71

TROYON (CONSTANTINE) .... Deceased

Cow in Pasture

9 x 7½

No. 72

LINDENSCHMIDT (PROF. WILHELM)..... Munich

Luther and Melancthon

24¼ x 19¼

No. 73

MOLITOR (P.)...............................Rome

St. Cecilia

31 x 18½

No. 74

MAGNUS (CAMILLE).......................Paris

Landscape

25½ x 32

No. 75

LATOUCHE (LOUIS) ....Deceased

Fishing-Boats at Bercke

21½ x 34½

No. 76

FROMENTIN (EUGÈNE)..................Deceased

Court-Yard

29 x 43½

No. 77

MORVILLIER ....

Landscape

30 x 54

No. 81. Adoration of the Goddess Minerva by the Maidens of Athens. Henri Le Roux.

No. 78

HEADE (M. J.)...................................New York

Lake George

26 x 50

No. 79

BROWN (GEO. L.)........................Deceased

Old Fisherman's Home, Amalfi

34 x 60

No. 80

DORÉ (GUSTAVE)........................Deceased

Landscape

26 x 43½

No. 81

LE ROUX (HECTOR)........................Paris

Adoration of the Goddess Minerva by the
Maidens of Athens

35 x 54

SECOND EVENING'S SALE.

FRIDAY, MARCH EIGHTH, AT CHICKERING HALL.

BEGINNING PROMPTLY AT EIGHT O'CLOCK.

No. 82

JACQUE (CHARLES ÉMILE).................Paris

* Sheep in Pasture

$5\frac{1}{4} \times 8\frac{3}{4}$

No. 83

BERTIN (JEAN VICTOR).... ....Deceased

Entrance to St. Cloud

$9\frac{3}{4} \times 14\frac{1}{8}$

No. 84

STADEMANN ADOLF..................Munich

Moonlight on the Bay

7×22

No. 85

CHASE (WM. M.).......................New York

* Brooklyn Heights

$6\frac{1}{4} \times 9\frac{3}{4}$

No. 86

ANTIGNA J. P. A.,.................... ....Deceased

Head

12 x 15

No. 87

CABAT (LOUIS).............................Paris

Atalanta

9⅞ x 12¾

No. 88

DELAROCHE (PAUL .... Deceased

Music Lesson

15½ x 12¼

No. 89

HUNT (W. M.)........ .... Deceased

Hay Field

14 x 18

No. 90

BOUDIN (EUGÈNE) .... Paris

*Shipping at Havre

13 x 9½

No. 91

BONHEUR (JULIETTE) (MME. PEYROL).....Paris

Pastoral Scene

16 x 13

No. 92

TROYON (CONSTANTINE)...............Deceased

Forest Scene

16 x 13

No. 93

ROUSSEAU (THÉODORE) ....Deceased

The Rapids

8¾ x 13

No. 94

COROT (J. B. C.).............. ....Deceased

The Old Monastery

12¼ x 15½

No. 95

CONSTABLE (JOHN ....Deceased

The Castle Gate

12¼ x 10

No. 94. The Old Monastery. B

No. 96

DUPRÉ (JULES) .... Paris

"Fisherman's Home

9½ x 8

No. 97

FULLER (GEORGE .... Deceased

Boy's Head

24 x 20

No. 98

LAMBINET (ÉMILE .... Deceased

Effet du Soir, La Seine à Bougeval

17 x 29

No. 99

BONNINGTON (RICHARD PARKES) ..... Deceased

" French Port

18½ x 25

No. 100

BRADFORD (WM. .... New York

Fishing Vessels Among the Icebergs

18 x 30

No. 101

BOGGS (F. M. . . . . .Paris

Thames at Greenwich

18 x 25¾

No. 102

MICHEL (GEORGES, ...Deceased

Moonlight

27 x 38

No. 103

BEYSCHLAG (JULIUS ROBERT) . . . . .Munich

* Children's Picnic

27⅞ x 22

No. 104

GÉRÔME (J. L.) . . . . Paris

Quintus Curtius

21¼ x 30

No. 105

COROT (J. B. C.) . . . . .Deceased

* Oak Trees at Fontainebleau

19¼ x 25¼

No. 106

GÉRICAULT (J. L. A. THÉODORE .... .Deceased

*Stable Scene

20 x 24

No. 107

DIAZ (N. V............................Deceased

Flowers

18½ 15

No. 108

COURBET (GUSTAVE).... ....Deceased

*Landscape and Figure, near Ornans

20 x 25½

No. 109

HUNT W. M.).... ....Deceased

Newbury Pastures

23 x 33½

No. 110

LATOUCHE LOUIS ....Deceased

*Beach at Bercke

16½ x 20½

No. 111

BERTIN (VICTOR..................... ....Deceased

Landscape

19½ x 13

No. 112

DAUBIGNY (C. F.,.......................Deceased

On the Oise

10 x 17½

No. 113

DECAMPS (A. G.,....... ....Deceased

Passing by on the other Side

11½ x 15

No. 114

DELACROIX EUGÈNE, ...Deceased

The Martyrdom of St. Stephen

15, x 10½

No. 115

BONHEUR (JULIETTE) (MME. PEYROL).....Paris

Noon-tide Rest

12 x 18

No. 112. On the Oise. C. F. Daubigny.

No. 116

ROUSSEAU (THÉODORE)................Deceased

*Eventide

8 x 13¾

No. 117

PLASSAN (ANTOINE ÉMILE)................Paris

Mother and Child

7 x 5¼

No. 118

DAUBIGNY (C. F.)......................Deceased

Sunset

8¼ x 13¾

No. 119

ROUSSEAU (THÉODORE)...... ....Deceased

*Landscape near the Village of La Brie

11¾ x 17¾

No. 120

TROYON (CONSTANTINE)...............Deceased

*Landscape, Cattle and Windmill

15 x 20¼

4

No. 121

COROT (J. B. C.)........................Deceased

* Landscape

16¼ x 21½

No. 122

DIAZ N. V.)..........................Deceased

Mother and Child

16 x 25¾

No. 123

GUILLAUMET (GUSTAVE)..................Paris

In the Vosges

15 x 21

No. 124

MAGNUS (CAMILLE).......................Paris

Forest Interior

12¼ x 9¾

No. 125

MARILHAT (PROSPER)...... ....Deceased

Roman Aqueduct with the Atlas Mountains in the Distance

10¼ x 16¼

No. 12. The Coming Storm. Constable.

No. 18 Battery Ridge ... Gall... ...

No. 139. The Triumph of Calvary. See Inness.

No. 126

DAUBIGNY (C. F.).. ....Deceased

Summary Landscape

10 x 16

No. 127

CONSTABLE (JOHN) ....Deceased

* The Coming Storm

15½ x 22

No. 128

ISABEY (LOUIS EUGÈNE)............... Deceased

Brittany Village

16¼ x 23¼

No. 129

INNESS (GEORGE) ....New York

The Triumph of Calvary

20 x 30

No. 130

COURBET (GUSTAVE) ....Deceased

* Winter Landscape

21½ x 26

No. 131

HUNT (W. M.) .... Deceased

* Head

22 x 18

No. 132

DECAMPS (A. G.) .... Deceased

Good Samaritan

18¼ x 25½

No. 133

COROT (J. B. C.) .... Deceased

Landscape, Provence

No. 134

DAUBIGNY (C. F.) .... Deceased

* Mill and Landscape

9½ x 17¼

No. 135

MILLET (J. F.) .... Deceased

Lessiveuse

15¼ x 10⅞

No. 32. Gul i Samartan. A. G. Decimas.

Millet.   KURTZ

No. 19. Goose Girl. J. F. Millet.

No. 11. Ploughing. Constantine Troop.

No. 137   A Summer's M   B.C.

No. 136

ROUSSEAU (THÉODORE).............Deceased

Cattle in Stable

13½ x 25¾

No. 137

TROYON (CONSTANTINE).............Deceased

Ploughing

21½ x 26

No. 138

ISABEY (LOUIS EUGÈNE).............Deceased

* Launching the Boat

18 x 25

No. 139

MILLET (J. F.)...........................Deceased

* Flight Into Egypt

12¾ x 9¾

No. 140

COROT (J. B. C.).......................Deceased

A Summer's Morning

26 x 19

No. 141

HUNT (W. M.) ....Deceased

* Head

20 x 16

No. 142

MICHEL (GEORGES)... ....Deceased

* Sunset

15 x 18½

No. 143

VAN MARCKE (ÉMILE ....Paris

Study of Cow

14 x 18

No. 144

VOLLON (ANTOINE)................ ....Paris

Studio Interior

22 x 18½

No. 145

VERNET (HORACE).....................Deceased

Head

10½ x 10

No. 42. The Charge. Eugène Fromentin.

No. 146

MEYER VON BREMEN.................Deceased

Writing a Letter

8 x 6

No. 147

WILKIE (SIR DAVID).................Deceased

Figures

7½ x 11½

No. 148

ZIEM (FELIX).........................Paris

Public Gardens, Venice

9½ x 32

No. 149

FROMENTIN (EUGÈNE)...............Deceased.

The Charge

22¼ x 35

No. 150

MAGNUS (CAMILLE,....................Paris

*Landscape

20 x 36

No. 151

LATOUCHE (LOUIS).................... ...Deceased

* Fisherman at Bercke

26 x 36

No. 152

SCHEFFER (ARY) ....Deceased

Revolution of 1830, Paris

33 x 37½

No. 153

BERTIN (VICTOR) ....Deceased

Roman Landscape with Cattle

(From the Duchess de Berri Collection.)

25½ x 35½

No. 154

DUPRÉ (JULES)............................Paris

Early Morning on the Coast

31¾ x 39¼

No. 155

JACQUE (CHARLES) ÉMILE ....Paris

* Mountain Flock

28½ x 39¼

No. 174   Pl. V.

No. 156. Mountain Flock, C. E. ___

No. 156

PERRAULT (LÉON) .... Paris

The Mendicants

43¼ x 32

No. 157

SCHEFFER (ARY) ....:.......... Deceased

Magdalen at the Foot of the Cross

39½ x 24½

No. 158

MÉLIN (JOSEPH) .... Deceased

Relais Volant

50 x 35

(Salon, 1885.)

No. 159

TERRY... ....

Tobit and Tobias

59 x 69½

AMERICAN ART ASSOCIATION,

MANAGERS.